Norway

Deborah Kopka

Carolrhoda Books, Inc. / Minneapolis

Photo Acknowledgments

Photographs and artwork are used courtesy of: John Erste, pp. 1, 2–3, 12–13, 14–15, 21 (bottom), 32–33, 38, 40, 42–43; Royal Norwegian Consulate General, pp. 4, 14, 23, 30 (bottom), 32, 34, 37, 40, 41 (both); Laura Westlund, pp. 5, 21 (top), 45; © Blaine Harrington III, pp. 6 (top), 8, 10, 12, 16, 17 (right), 22, 24, 26 (top), 27, 28, 29 (top), 33 (bottom); TRIP/J. Merryweather, p. 6 (bottom); © Kay Shaw, p. 7; © B & C Alexander, pp. 9, 11 (both), 13, 18, 19 (both), 29 (bottom), 30 (top), 31 (top), 35; © Ric Ergenbright Photography/Floyd Norgaard, p. 15; TRIP/D. Saunders, pp. 17 (left), 31 (bottom); TRIP/M. Jenkin, p. 20; Jetty St. John, p. 25; Peer Rødal Haugen, p. 26 (bottom); The Norwegian Information Service, p. 33 (top); TRIP/GV Press, p. 36; TRIP/R. Etter, p. 38; Steve Foley/Independent Picture Service, p. 39; The Nobel Foundation, p. 44. Cover photo © B & C Alexander.

Carolrhoda Books, Inc.
A division of Lerner Publishing Group
241 First Avenue North
Minneapolis, Minnesota 55401 U.S.A.

Website address: www.lernerbooks.com

Words in bold type are explained in a glossary that begins on page 44.

Library of Congress Cataloging-in-Publication Data

Kopka, Deborah L.
Norway / by Deborah Kopka.
    p.   cm. — (A ticket to)
  Includes bibliographical references and index.
  Summary: Briefly describes the people, geography, government, religion, language, customs, and lifestyles of Norway.
    ISBN 1–57505–148–6 (lib. bdg.: alk. paper)
    1. Norway—Juvenile literature. [1. Norway.] I. Title. II Series:
DL409.K67   2001b   99–050689
948.1—dc21

Manufactured in the United States of America
1 2 3 4 5 6 – JR – 06 05 04 03 02 01

Contents

Welcome!

A bridge connects a small island to the Norwegian mainland.

Norwegians call their country *Norge*, which means "the way to the North." It is easy to tell why! Norway is the northernmost country on the **continent** of Europe.

Norway arches over the top of Finland to meet the Russian Federation. Sweden sweeps along eastern Norway. The Norwegian Sea, part of the Atlantic Ocean, is on the west. Southward spreads the North Sea. An arm of the North Sea called the Skagerrak separates Norway and Denmark.

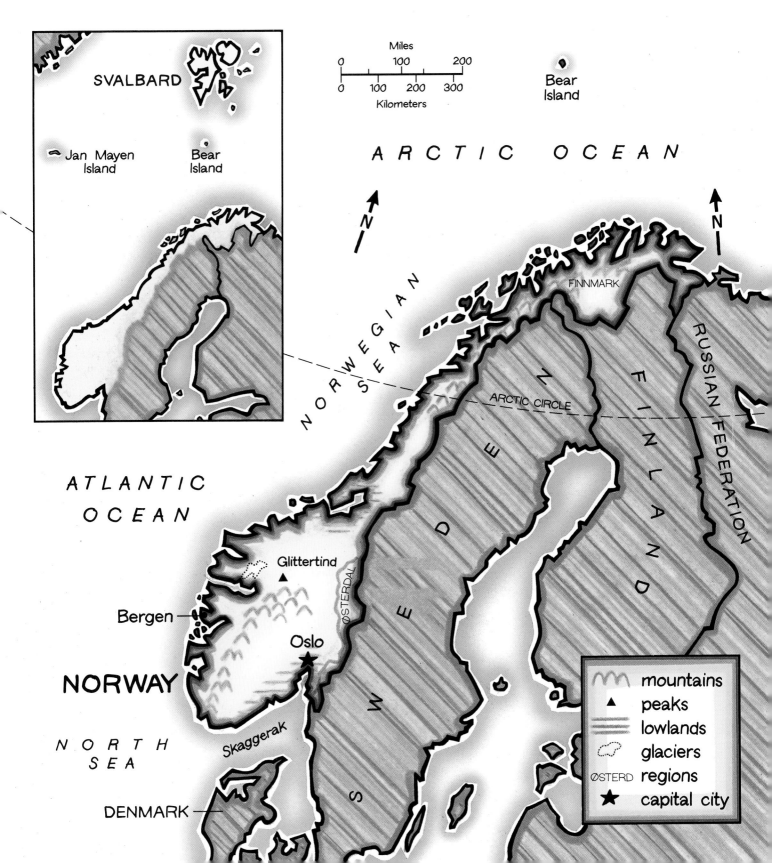

Mountains and Fjords

Mountains (right) *are parts of the earth's surface that rise high into the sky. This glacier* (below) *lies on Norway's western coast.*

Norway is a good place to find mountain ranges. Deep valleys separate mountains with forested or rocky slopes. High in the mountains are huge ice fields called glaciers.

The mountains slope into the sea in western Norway. Deep canyons called **fjords** lead from the sea into the countryside. Norway's fjords make the coastline look wrinkled.

Care to row your boat across this fjord? Some fjords are so big that large ships can travel them!

Rolling farmland and forests are common sights in Norway.

Heading Downhill

Most Norwegians live in southeastern Norway. Thick forests carpet the Østerdal, Norway's longest and easternmost valley.

Map Whiz Quiz

Check out the **map** on page 5! Trace Norway with a crayon. Find the Norwegian Sea. Mark it with a W for West. Now find Sweden. Mark it with an E for East. Now trace the line of the Arctic Circle. Put an N, for North, above the Arctic Circle.

Keep heading south! You will hit Oslo, the **capital** of Norway. Oslo has forests and lakes that citizens love to visit.

Homes sit near a hilly forest in south central Norway.

Finnmark

From May to September, the sun always shines in Finnmark. That is why it is nicknamed the Land of the Midnight Sun.

The Arctic Circle cuts through Norway. This imaginary line marks off a circle around the North Pole, the world's northernmost point. Finnmark, or northernmost Norway, lies high

The colorful northern lights can sometimes be seen in northern Norway.

A full moon rises over a snowy Finnmark landscape.

in the Arctic Circle. Being so close to the North Pole means that, in Finnmark, days and nights can last for months.

Norwegians spend a sunny day at an outdoor café in Oslo.

How's the Weather?

Western, southern, and inland Norway share a **temperate climate.** In the summer, temperatures range between 60 and 72 degrees. And in the wintertime, temperatures do not drop far below 15 degrees. But it is

colder in northern and eastern Norway. When winter snows fall, Norwegians do not mind. It gives them a chance to get out their skis!

The ocean freezes over near the Svalbard, Norway's northernmost islands.

A Long History

Norway's early people left these carvings.
What do you think the symbols mean?

People have lived in Norway for thousands of years. Early Norwegians were herders, fishers, and farmers. Around the year A.D. 800, the Viking culture appeared. Vikings were

Viking longboats are a world-famous symbol of Norway.

skilled craftspeople, warriors, and traders. They journeyed thousands of miles in their ships. Vikings also raided across Europe.

From 1030 to 1380, Norway was a unified kingdom. From 1380 to 1814 Norway was a part of Denmark. Then in 1814 Norway united with Sweden. In 1905 Norway became an independent nation.

Most Norwegians have light-colored skin, hair, and eyes, like these brothers.

The Norwegians

In each region of Norway, people have a different *bunad* (national costume). Norwegians may wear their bunads on special occasions, such as holidays.

Most Norwegians
have blond hair and
blue eyes, although
some have brown
hair or brown eyes.

Do you like this Norwegian woman's bunad?

Two dancers wear their bunads for a special occasion.

People from Asia,
Africa, and South
America also live
in Norway.

The Sami

About 30,000 members of the Sami (Lapp) **ethnic group** live in Norway. Finnmark is their traditional home. The Sami may have been Norway's first people.

A young Sami girl wears a traditional outfit for a holiday.

Many Sami work as farmers, loggers, or fishers. If parents choose a modern lifestyle, Sami kids live, dress, and go to school like other Norwegian kids.

Some Sami wear traditional clothes every day. Most Sami only put on traditional clothing for special occasions.

Some Sami herd reindeer for a living.

A very small number of Sami live in tents made of reindeer hide.

Do you like fish? Norwegians sure do. Many Norwegian meals include fish.

Let's Eat

Many Norwegians like to eat big breakfasts of cereal, meat, herring, cheese, and buttered bread with jam. At lunchtime workers and schoolchildren pull out a tasty *smørbrød* or two brought from home. Smørbrøds are open-face sandwiches. In the evening, people eat filling dinners, such as meat, fish, and potatoes.

On special occasions, Norwegians have buffet meals. At a buffet, people choose what they like from heaping platters of meat, seafood, cheeses, and wafer-thin bread.

Dear Penny:

Norway is cool! Dad rented a boat today. He steered us around little islands that poke out of the ocean. And then he let me steer! It was a lot of fun.

Wish you were here!

Lucy

Do you think these fishermen are speaking Bokmål or Nynorsk?

Bokmål or Nynorsk?

The Norwegian language has two official versions, which are called Bokmål and Nynorsk. Outside major cities, you'll hear

many local Norwegian **dialects.**
Norwegians can understand anyone who
speaks and reads Bokmål, Nynorsk, or a local
dialect. But Norwegians cannot understand
the Sami language without having learned it.

Norwegians use Bokmål and Nynorsk in newspapers, books, and magazines, on the radio, and on television.

Children wear the funny hats they made at their Oslo kindergarten.

School

Norwegian children start first grade the year they turn seven. Students in grades one through six don't receive grades. But they still have to study! Twice a year, their teachers send home progress reports.

Teachers grade students in grades seven through nine twice a year.

During grades four through six, students have classes in Norwegian, religion, math, English, social studies, and music. All pupils study Sami history and culture.

Small Schools

Because many Norwegian children live in tiny villages, small schools dot the countryside. Of the 3,000 schools in Norway, 650 have fewer than 30 students each!

Kids

Many Norwegian parents work outside the home. When no parent is at home, a *dogmamma* (day mother) looks after

After school these kids (above) might go camping with a scout troop (left).

young children. A dogmamma is usually a family friend or a neighbor.

All in the Family

Here are the Norwegian words for family members. Practice using these terms on your own family. See if they understand you!

grandfather	*bestefar*	(BEHS-tuh-fahr)
grandmother	*bestemor*	(BEHS-tuh-moor)
father	*far*	(FAHR)
mother	*mor*	(MOOR)
uncle	*onkel*	(OHNG-kuhl)
aunt	*tante*	(TUHN-tuh)
brother	*bror*	(BROOR)
sister	*søster*	(SOOHR-stuhr)

Can you name the members of this Norwegian boy's family?

Buildings

Cozy, brightly painted houses dot Norway's countryside. Homes are tucked into valleys, or they overlook lakes and fjords. City dwellers might rent apartments in large buildings.

Some Norwegians live in tall houses.

Norway's most famous architecture has been around for a long time. Norwegians built stave churches in the Middle Ages. Some stave churches are 1,000 years old.

Wood carvers decorated stave churches (above) *with dragons, vines, and leaves. Each stave church is different. But most of the houses in this town in the Svalbard* (left) *look the same.*

Hit the Slopes!

Norwegian children are said to be "born with skis on their feet." Tots start skiing at age two or three. At the same

In the wintertime, Norwegian kids love to ski (above). *And in the summertime, soccer is a favorite sport* (right).

Kids whiz downhill on a sled.

Biking is a great way to see Norway's forests.

age, kids usually learn how to skate and sled.

Norwegians often like to be outdoors in the summertime, too. Folks fish in fjords, lakes, and streams. Boats zip around Norway's coasts. Many Norwegians enjoy hiking in the country's national forests.

Keep the Beat!

Many Norwegians love to strike up the band.

Norwegians love music! Students learn a musical instrument, such as the violin, trumpet, or flute. School bands perform on Constitution Day.

Children and adults enjoy jazz and rock music, too. They turn on the radio to catch the songs of favorite Norwegian pop groups, such as the Dum Dum Boys.

Edvard Grieg

Edvard Grieg (1843–1907) used harmonies from Norwegian folk tunes when he composed his own music. In modern times, music lovers honor Grieg as one of the greatest composers of all time.

A pair of musicians spend some time practicing. They also earn coins from passersby who like the tune!

The Church of Norway

The official church of Norway is the Lutheran church. About 90 percent of

Norwegians go to church for weekly services or for traditional religious holidays.

A Sami baby receives a blessing as a relative holds the child.

Norwegians are Lutheran. But Norwegians may choose to follow any religion.

A baby joins the Church of Norway through **baptism.** After the service, guests gather for a fancy lunch. The baby receives gifts, such as a first Bible.

Celebrating Holidays

A boy and his mother wrap presents for Christmas.

On June 23, the longest day of the year, Norwegians celebrate Midsummer Night. People in each neighborhood light a huge bonfire and honor the day with singing, dancing, and feasting.

On Christmas Eve (December 24), most Norwegians go to church.

Afterwards families gather for a big meal. Save room for cookies and treats, such as a tower cake called *kransekake.* After eating dinner, folks gather around a Christmas tree to open gifts!

Constitution Day

On May 17 each year, the country celebrates Constitution Day. This celebration includes a children's procession. Thousands of children in every city and town dress in their bunads. Both children and adults enjoy sports, games, and magic shows.

A woman holds handmade, hand-decorated items. Her clothes are homemade, too.

Made by Hand

Norwegians can just head to the store to buy what they need. But many choose to make things. They might carve wooden furniture or weave rugs. Some knit fancy sweaters with beautiful snowflake patterns. Many Norwegians have handmade bunads.

Make a Clove Ball!

Many Norwegian kids like to make crafts at Christmastime. Here's a favorite! The spicy scent will last long after the orange has dried.

You will need:

1 large fresh navel orange
1 cup of whole cloves

1. Wash off the orange with a damp kitchen towel. Allow the orange to sit at room temperature for one hour.

2. Gently push the cloves into the orange, one at a time. Work on one small area, and then move to the next one until you have covered the entire orange.

Grab a Book!

Norwegians love to curl up with a book. Lots of people choose exciting best-sellers. Many also pick books from Norway's past.

In the late 1800s, some Norwegians became famous writers. Bjørnstjerne Bjørnson wrote stories, novels, poetry, plays, and the words to the Norwegian national anthem.

Sigrid Undset wrote *Kristin Lavransdatter*, a

People around the world still enjoy the plays of Henrik Ibsen.

Knut Hamsun (below) *wrote a famous book called* The Growth of the Soil.

Sigrid Undset's work has been translated into many languages.

book about a Norwegian girl who lived long ago. Norway's most famous playwright, Henrik Ibsen, wrote 25 plays.

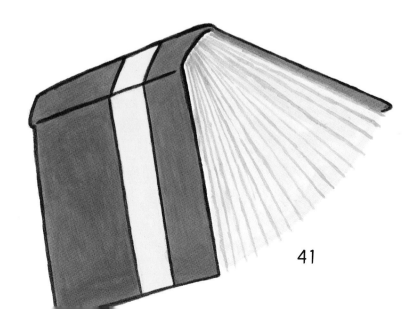

Story Time

"Once upon a time" is a phrase that starts lots of Norwegian **folktales.** Families passed the stories down through the years. The stories often teach a lesson about life. Other tales tell of people or talking animals who outsmart dangerous creatures.

Three Billy Goats Gruff

Once upon a time, a small goat skipped over a bridge leading to a grassy meadow. But a troll living under the bridge wanted to eat the goat. The goat begged the troll to wait. A bigger goat would be a better meal! So the troll let the little goat pass to the grassy meadow. Soon a medium-size goat trotted along the bridge. The goat told the troll to wait to eat his even bigger brother. The troll agreed. Soon a huge goat with giant horns thundered across the bridge. Onto the bridge the troll jumped, ready for his feast. But the large goat used his horns to toss the troll off the bridge. Then the goat joined his brothers in the meadow.

New Words to Learn

baptism: A Christian ceremony that brings people into the religion by sprinkling them with, or immersing them in, water.

capital: A city where the government is located.

continent: One of the six or seven great divisions of land on the globe.

dialect: A regional variety of language that has different pronunciations from other regional varieties of the same language.

ethnic group: A group of people with many things in common, such as language, religion, and customs.

The Nobel Prize

Alfred Nobel (1833–1896) was the Swedish inventor of dynamite. He founded the Nobel Peace Prize. The Storting (Norway's legislature) awards the prize to people and groups who help world unity and peace.

Norway's Flag

Norway's red flag has a blue and white cross.

fjord: A narrow inlet from the ocean. Steep cliffs often bound fjords.

folktale: A timeless story told by word of mouth from grandparent to parent to child. Many folktales have been written down in books.

map: A drawing or chart of all or part of the earth or sky.

temperate climate: Year-round weather that is neither extremely hot nor extremely cold.

New Words to Say

Bjørnstjerne	BYUHRNS-tyehr-neh
Bjørnson	BYUHRN-sohn
Bokmål	BOOK-mahwl
bunad	BOO-nahd
dogmamma	DAHG-mah-mah
Edvard Grieg	EHD-vahrd GRIHG
fjord	FYAHRD
Henrik Ibsen	HEHN-rihk IHP-sehn
kransekake	KRAHN-seh-kah-keh
Norge	NAWR-geh
Nynorsk	NEE-nohshk
Østerdal	UHS-tehr-dahl
Sigrid Undset	ZIHG-rihd EWN-seht
Skagerrak	SKAH-geh-rahk
smørbrød	SMUHR-bruhr
Svalbard	SFAHL-bahr

More Books to Read

Charbonneau, Claudette, and Patricia Slade Lander. *The Land and People of Norway.* New York: HarperCollins Publishers, 1992.

Gascoyne, David. *Let's Visit Norway.* London: Burke Publishing Company Limited, 1984.

Haviland, Virginia. *Favorite Fairy Tales Told in Norway.* Boston: Little, Brown and Company, 1961.

Lye, Keith. *Take a Trip to Norway.* London: Franklin Watts, 1984.

Pitkänen, Matti A. *Grandchildren of the Vikings.* Minneapolis: Carolrhoda Books, 1996.

St. John, Jetty. *A Family in Norway.* Minneapolis: Lerner Publications Company, 1988.

New Words to Find